CREATIVE
HANDMADE PAPER

To Bob

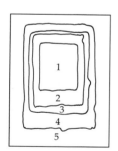

Front cover: *a selection of handmade papers. 1. Recycled tissue dyed with tea-bags. 2. Recycled paper and straw dyed with lemon verbena tea. 3. Cotton rag paper. 4. Recycled paper and red maple leaves. 5. Recycled paper and grass cuttings.*

Back cover: *cover illustration for a spring issue of* Watchword *magazine.*
This landscape is made from grass and recycled Christmas wrapping papers.

CREATIVE HANDMADE PAPER

How to make
paper from recycled and
natural materials

DAVID WATSON

SEARCH PRESS

First published in Great Britain 1991
Search Press Limited,
Wellwood, North Farm Road,
Tunbridge Wells, Kent TN2 3DR

Reprinted 1992, 1993, 1994, 1996

The basic technique of making recycled paper, demonstrated by
David Watson, is taken from *How to make your own Recycled Paper*
by Malcolm Valentine, also published by Search Press.

The author would like to thank Maureen Richardson for inspiring
him to work with paper; Shirley Chubb for permission to use the
papers on pages 11 and 59, which were produced during their
joint residency at the Institute of Education, London; Tom
Embleton and the textile students from Northbrook College,
Worthing, for permission to use the three-dimensional items
shown on page 69; *New Scientist* magazine for permission to
reproduce the artwork on page 72; and *The Sunday Times* for
permission to reproduce the artwork on the back cover.

If you have difficulty in obtaining any of the materials or equipment mentioned in this book, then please write for further
information to the Publishers, Search Press Ltd., Wellwood,
North Farm Road, Tunbridge Wells, Kent TN2 3DR.

ISBN 0 85532 730 8 (Pb)
ISBN 0 85532 712 X (C)

Composition by Genesis Typesetting, Rochester, Kent
Colour Separation by P&W Graphics Pte Ltd, Singapore
Printed in Spain by A.G. Elkar, S. Coop. - 48012 Bilbao

Contents

Introduction

How many different types of paper can you recognize? Possibly, you can name quite a few, such as recycled paper, manila, and cotton rag. Alternatively, you may be tempted to name the paper according to its associated function, e.g. computer paper, writing paper, wallpaper and newspaper. If the same question were asked of a Japanese person, then he or she would probably respond quite differently and be able to list a whole range of plant papers. The list may start with *washi*, the traditional name for Japanese papers, and then follow on to describe *kozo* papers, which are made from *gampi*, hemp and *mitsumata* plants.

The prime difference illustrated here is that in the western world we have recently acquired most of our raw materials for paper production from wood pulp, and depending on its intended use the paper is treated with various additives in order to improve strength, durability and texture. In comparison, the Japanese have a long and continuing tradition of various plant materials being used as the raw material in the papermaking process. All of these plants produce different papers with varying degrees of strength, durability, texture, opacity, colour and weight. Accordingly, it is the intended function of the paper that determines the plant to be used as the raw material.

The Japanese were not the first to discover papermaking. Over 5000 years ago the Egyptians were making a type of paper from the stem pith of papyrus, a tall aquatic plant that grows on the banks of the river Nile. The stems of the reeds were split, woven, and then dampened and beaten into flat sheets, which were polished smooth with stones. Some of these papyrus sheets, or rolls, can still be seen today, their beautiful illustrations barely dimmed by the passage of time, preserved for centuries by the dry climate of Egypt.

The Greeks and Romans continued making and using papyrus, but true paper as we know it was invented by the Chinese and patented by Ts'ai Lun, an Imperial Court official, in AD105. At first, he used ropes and old fishing nets to make his paper. These he beat to a pulp with water, before draining and pressing the pulp into sheets which he dried in the sun before use. Later, he started using plant fibres and also silk threads. As well as these materials the Chinese used rags in their papermaking process. Today, some early examples of Chinese paper can still be seen in the British Museum.

With a little research, it is possible to find many contemporary examples of handmade paper in use today, all produced from traditional materials such as cotton rag. The purpose of this book is to help you develop an appreciation of the natural qualities of handmade paper, by guiding you through the process of making your own. Throughout, I have tried to keep the instructions simple and easy to follow and, whenever possible, I have used equipment and materials which can be located easily and obtained without too much effort.

Like the Japanese, we too have an abundance of plant and other materials which are suitable for making paper, such as the fluff from laundry drying machines, vegetable peelings, grass cuttings and nettles, not to mention the endless supplies of discarded papers which can be recycled. Most of these materials can be acquired free of charge, the only cost being the time and effort involved in collecting and preparing them. All of them will create a different type of paper, each with its own characteristics and suitable for different purposes. During my own research into papermaking I have experimented with a vast range of raw materials and, frequently, have enjoyed surprising results.

I hope that by following the course of this book you will begin to understand the principles behind the papermaking process and also, with a fair degree of confidence, be able to use your immediate environment to locate the necessary materials from which to make your paper. In my view, the production of handmade paper is far more than a rewarding craft activity. I see it developing as an important medium of creativity that can help to counteract the surge of environmental damage and raw material misuse that affects us presently.

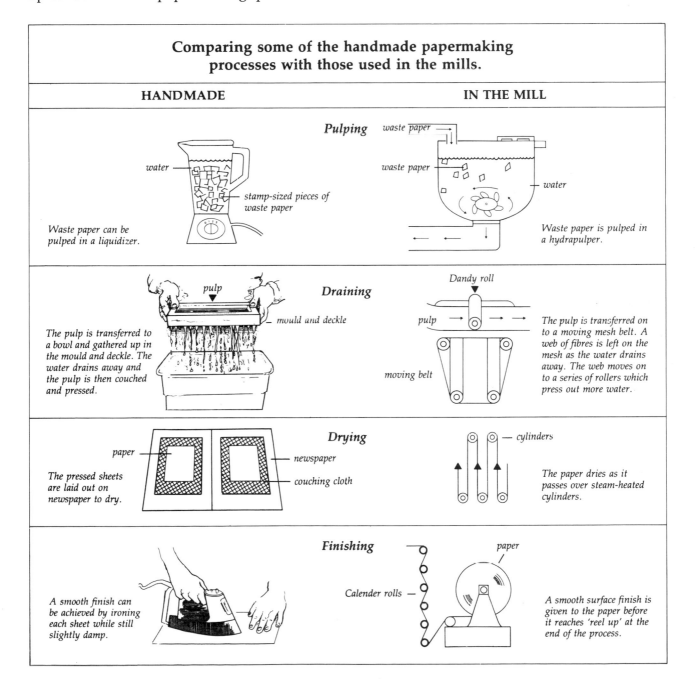

Comparing some of the handmade papermaking processes with those used in the mills.

HANDMADE	IN THE MILL

Pulping

water — stamp-sized pieces of waste paper

Waste paper can be pulped in a liquidizer.

waste paper

waste paper — water

Waste paper is pulped in a hydrapulper.

Draining

pulp — mould and deckle

The pulp is transferred to a bowl and gathered up in the mould and deckle. The water drains away and the pulp is then couched and pressed.

Dandy roll

pulp — moving belt

The pulp is transferred on to a moving mesh belt. A web of fibres is left on the mesh as the water drains away. The web moves on to a series of rollers which press out more water.

Drying

paper — newspaper — couching cloth

The pressed sheets are laid out on newspaper to dry.

cylinders

The paper dries as it passes over steam-heated cylinders.

Finishing

A smooth finish can be achieved by ironing each sheet while still slightly damp.

paper

Calender rolls

A smooth surface finish is given to the paper before it reaches 'reel up' at the end of the process.

HOW
TO MAKE
RECYCLED
PAPERS

How to make recycled papers

Because it is in such abundant supply and is so inexpensive, we think nothing of discarding paper once it has been used, and vast amounts of reclaimable waste paper are thrown away each year. The next time that you are about to throw out some used paper, just stop and think. With relatively little expense you could recycle it and produce your own sheets of handmade paper, combining the pleasure of creating something original with the satisfaction of utilizing waste materials.

Equipment and materials

Nearly all the equipment and materials required for making paper can be found around the home, apart from the mould and deckle. The list below is followed by a full description of each of the items needed.

Waste paper
Newspaper or absorbent paper
Mould and deckle
Liquidizer, or bucket and long, thick piece of
  wood
Oblong washing-up bowl or small water tank
Shallow oblong tray
Smooth, reusable kitchen cloths
Two pressing boards 25 × 20cm (10 × 8in)
Palette knife
Clothes iron, optional

Pages 8–9: a selection of recycled papers made from waste materials such as newspapers, old shirts, Christmas wrapping paper, computer paper, tissue paper, etching paper, cardboard, and fluff from laundry drying machines.

Opposite: stacks of recycled papers.

Waste paper

When you recycle paper, the waste paper itself is your raw material. Being the starting point in the process, your raw material is probably the most important factor in determining the characteristics of the final paper produced. If you use a poor quality paper such as newsprint as the raw material, then the paper that is produced from it is likely to be of a slightly lower grade than the original newsprint. Newsprint not only yellows very quickly but also becomes brittle in a short period of time, and your recycled paper will inherit these qualities.

Generally, there is an abundance of waste papers which are suitable for recycling. Old newspapers are acceptable to start with as they are readily available, and they are very absorbent which makes them easy to break down into a pulp. Do not stay with them for too long though, as with only a little more effort better qualities of paper can be obtained from discarded photocopier paper, computer paper and blotting paper. If you can get hold of old watercolour paper or etching paper, then you will find that the recycled paper produced will be much stronger and more durable than that from a lower grade paper. Some glossy magazines and plastic-coated papers do not react well to the recycling process and are difficult to break down in a liquidizer or by hand, so these are best avoided at first. It is also worth remembering that any paper containing ink will discolour when it is recycled, due to the ink mixing with the pulp.

I have produced many recycled papers on which it is possible to write, type, and photocopy. Some are even suitable for use in a

word processor. However, it must be stressed that papers produced by the recycling process will always end up being extremely absorbent and some fibres may separate from the main sheet when handling. This means that when using the paper in conjunction with machinery increased amounts of cleaning may be necessary. Later in the book there is a section on strengthening and sizing the paper to make it less absorbent (see pages 44–47). Try out these techniques once you have acquired some degree of success at making and drying your sheets of recycled paper.

As well as waste paper for pulping, you will require a supply of absorbent paper or clean newspaper to make your couching mound (see pages 16–17).

Mould and deckle

This simple device is an essential part of the papermaking process and is available from craft shops and suppliers. However, it is relatively easy to make your own and instructions are given here.

The mould is comprised of a rectangular frame across which is stretched a layer of mesh. The deckle is the same size as the mould and is an open frame which rests on top of the mesh-covered mould. The wet pulp is deposited onto the mesh before it is pressed and dried into sheets of paper.

Materials 180cm (6ft) length of 2cm (¾in) square wood cut into four 25cm (10in) lengths and four 20cm (8in) lengths; nylon mesh (curtain netting or similar) with between 12 to 20 holes per cm (50 holes per in); brass or stainless steel pins, or staples; waterproof adhesive; nails.

Method Arrange the cut wood to make two frames of the same size and shape. If you have the necessary equipment and knowledge, then the corners can be mitred. Alternatively, they can be fixed with brass corner plates, or glued together with waterproof adhesive and secured with nails.

The mesh must be stretched tightly over the top of one of the frames. It is very important that this is as tight as possible. Nylon stretches when wet so dampen the mesh before stretching it. To obtain a tight tension, firstly pin the mesh to the middle of one outside edge, then to the middle of the opposite outside edge, pulling as you pin. Pin the middles of the two remaining edges. When all four sides are secured, begin working outwards towards each corner, pulling the mesh tight as you fix each pin into the wood. Curtain netting tends to sag after a while, but it can be supported with threads which are stretched across under the mesh.

Finish by trimming away any excess mesh. The mesh-covered frame is the mould and the open frame is the deckle.

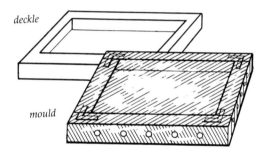

Other equipment

A liquidizer is ideal for pulping the waste paper. If you do not possess a liquidizer, then the paper can be pulped by hand. For this you will need a bucket and a long, thick piece of wood with which to pound the waste paper into fine particles. If you are using the hand method, then soak the paper for two hours before pounding. Remove some of the water and beat the paper to a slush pulp. This can take quite a long time and the resulting pulp should be fairly smooth. There is no need to soak the paper if you are using a liquidizer.

Once the paper is pulped it is poured into a bowl. In this section an ordinary plastic washing-up bowl is used, but any suitably sized oblong bowl will do.

Using the mould and deckle, the pulp is transferred onto a couching cloth. The term couching (pronounced 'cooching') simply refers to the process of transferring the pulp from the mould onto a clean, moist cloth. Smooth, synthetic kitchen cleaning cloths are ideal for this purpose. The couching cloths are used to cover each sheet of pulp as it is made. The sheets are layered between the couching cloths before pressing begins. Coarse cloths with holes are not recommended because they disturb and spoil the smooth finish of the recycled sheet. In this section the couching process is carried out in a shallow oblong plastic tray, but a flat working surface covered with plastic sheeting could be used just as well. The couching mound is simply made from newspaper or absorbent paper.

Pressure has to be applied to the wet sheets in order to expel the water, and two pressing boards are required for this purpose. One is positioned beneath the layered sheets, and one above, like a sandwich. The boards are squeezed together, slowly at first, pressing gently, then much harder to drain the water away. Make sure that you use strong boards that will not bend under pressure. Once they

are pressed, if the sheets are left to dry naturally, then they will have a rough surface. To obtain a smooth, even surface an iron will be required to press the sheets whilst they are still damp. The finished dry sheets of paper are removed from the couching cloths simply by peeling the two apart. If any difficulty is experienced in separating them, then a palette knife can be used to ease the edges apart first.

Many decorative and textural effects can be created by introducing colours and objects into the pulp in the initial stages of papermaking. These techniques are discussed in detail in the sections on texture (see pages 48–52) and dyeing (see pages 53–56), and are worth experimenting with once you have mastered the basic process of recycling paper.

Note When you have finished using a particular pulp do not throw it away or, worse still, put it down the sink (causing a blockage). Drain off the water using a sieve, squeeze the pulp together expelling all of the water, and save for later use.

A selection of materials required for making paper.

1 △

2 ▽

Making the pulp

1. Tear the paper into long narrow strips. You will need enough paper to fill the liquidizer approximately six times over.

2. Tear the strips into smaller stamp-sized pieces. Place a small handful of the torn paper into the liquidizer. You will need to fill the liquidizer two-thirds full of water. Blend the mixture for approximately thirty seconds, but not all at once. Stop the liquidizer after ten second intervals and allow it to rest, otherwise it may overheat or burn out.

3. Pour the pulp into a washing-up bowl half full of clean water. Repeat steps 1, 2 and 3 five times more.

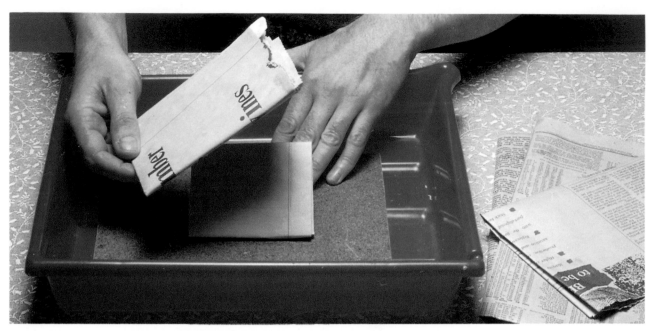

6 △

Making the couching mound

4. It is advisable at this stage to build up a simple couching mound which makes the task of transferring the pulp from the mesh-covered mould to the couching cloths a little easier. You will need a clean, shallow oblong tray. To make the mound, lay a pressing board in the base of the tray. Fold three sheets of paper into small, medium and large pieces. Using the pressing board as the base, layer up the folded sheets with the smallest on the bottom and the largest on top.

5. Pour water over the paper until it begins to take on the shape of a mound. Moisten it well as it needs to be fairly wet before the mound takes shape. Before starting to make the first sheet, place a damp couching cloth on top of the mound.

Moulding the sheets

6. It is important to stir up the pulp mixture vigorously and frequently so that the paper fibres do not settle at the bottom of the bowl. If this happens, then it will be difficult to create proper sheets. Now place the deckle on the top of the mould which should have its mesh side facing upwards.

17

7. With the deckle uppermost, hold the mould and deckle firmly on each of the short sides. Take them down into the pulp mixture at a forty-five degree angle, pulling them towards you as shown.

8. In one continuous movement level off the mould and deckle beneath the surface, then, keeping them level, pull them up out of the pulp mixture. The water will drain away through the mesh. While the pulp is still wet, gently shake the mould and deckle forwards, backwards and from side to side. This motion helps the fibres to settle. Do not continue the motion as the pulp becomes less runny; too much movement at this stage will affect the sheet as it forms.

9. A layer of pulp should cover the mesh. If this is too thin, then add more liquidized pulp to the bowl. Return the pulp covering the mesh to the bowl and repeat the steps until you reach this stage. Wait until all the water has drained away and remove the deckle. You are now ready to couch the first sheet.

19

Couching the sheets

10. Transfer the mould and deckle to the shallow tray and, with the pulp facing the mound, rest the mould on the edge of the cloth, holding the two short sides as shown.

11. In one continuous movement, *roll* the pulp firmly over the mound . . .

12. . . . and bring the bottom edge of the mould up, pressing the top edge into the cloth as you do so.

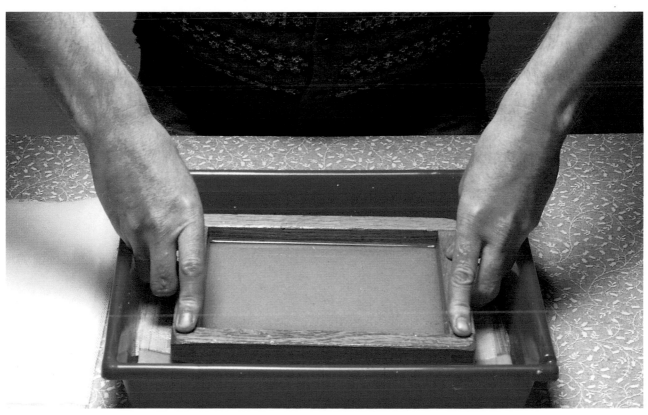

11 △

12 ▽

13 △

14 ▽

13. The pulp should adhere to the mound. If there are still areas of pulp sticking to the mesh, then the whole process of trapping and couching the pulp has to be repeated. The unsuccessful sheet can be simply washed off the mound and the cloth by laying each pulp-covered surface on top of the pulp in the bowl. Replace the used couching cloth with a clean damp one. Remoisten the mound before commencing.

14. Take another cloth and place it on top of the sheet of pulp. Smooth out any wrinkles or these will be forced into the pulp during the pressing process and the crease marks will be visible on the final surface. Repeat steps 6 to 14 and continue layering the damp cloths and sheets of pulp. Up to ten sheets can be made at a time. If the pulp becomes thinner as it is removed from the bowl, then add more liquidized pulp to the mixture.

Pressing the sheets

15. When the layering is complete, cover the final sheet with a couching cloth and place the second pressing board on top. You now have a sandwich with the two pressing boards top and bottom and the layers of pulp in between.

16 △

16. Turn the whole stack over. Remove your couching mound and replace it with a folded sheet of dry newspaper. Firmly squeeze the two boards together to expel as much water as possible. The newspaper will absorb most of the excess water as it is forced out of the pulp. Alternatively, a good way to squeeze out the water is to stand on top of the pile. This is better done outside, but if you are going to use this method inside, then spread plenty of newspaper over the floor first!

17. Remove the top pressing board and carefully peel off each cloth.

18. The pulp will hold together at this stage without slipping. By now the fibres will have joined to form a flexible sheet of paper. The sheets are still wet, however, and they will require a drying period.

19 △

20 ▽

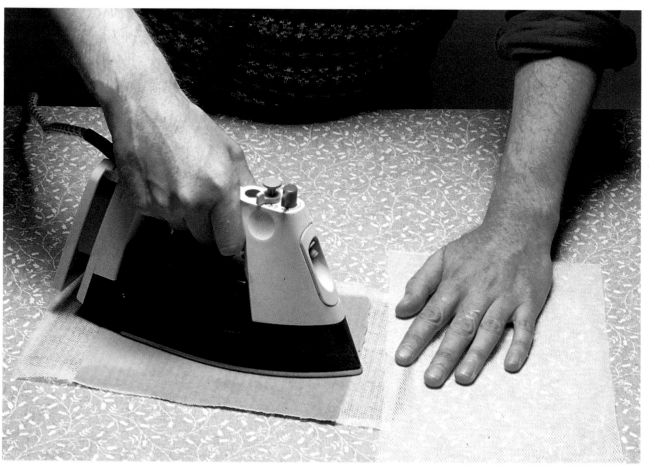

21 △

Drying the sheets

19. Lay out the sheets (still on their couching cloths) on several layers of newspaper and leave them until they are dry. This can take from six hours to one day in normal room temperature. A sunny window-ledge will speed up the process. You can also try hanging the cloths on a washing line, preferably indoors, but perhaps outside with close supervision if it is a windless day.

Finishing off

20. You may prefer your paper to have a rough surface, in which case just leave the sheets to dry out completely before removing them from the couching cloth. Otherwise, to achieve a smooth, even finish, simply iron each sheet while it is still slightly damp.

21. Only remove the sheet from the couching cloth when it is completely dry. Gently peel it away from the cloth as shown. It should come away quite easily, but if you experience any difficulty, then use a palette knife to ease the edges apart before starting to peel.

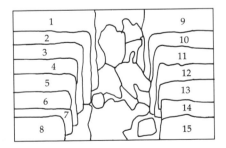

Pages 28–29: a variety of materials can be added to recycled paper pulp in order to achieve a decorative effect.
1. Grass. 2. Hay. 3. Straw. 4. Wool. 5. Hair. 6. Seaweed.
7. Plant mixture. 8. Red satin fibres. 9. Straw.
10. Dried leaves. 11. Petals. 12. Tea-bags. 13. Red satin fibres.
14. Wool. 15. Red plastic fibres.

HOW
TO MAKE
PLANT
PAPERS

Above: papers from fruit and vegetable
materials.
1,2,3. Potato plants. 4. Cabbage
leaves. 5. Dried vine leaves.
6. Bananas.

Pages 30–31: *a selection of plant papers made from materials
such as seaweed, potato plants, bamboo leaves, pampas-grass
heads, thistles, blossom, and a general hedgerow mixture.*

How to make plant papers

As well as recycling waste paper, it is possible to make your own paper from plant materials. There is a vast array available, ranging from grass cuttings and nettles through to bamboo leaves and seaweed, all of which will produce different papers with individual characteristics. In the papermaking process, the main difference between using waste paper as the raw material and using plant material is the method by which the pulp is produced. Waste paper is pulped by pounding it with a stick, or liquidizing it, in water. In comparison, plant material must first be broken down before it can be pounded or liquidized into a smooth pulp. This breaking-down process is achieved by boiling the plant in an alkaline solution and then washing it thoroughly.

Equipment and materials

All of the equipment and materials needed to make plant papers are listed here. Most of the items required are common to both the production of plant papers and recycled papers, and if you have tried the recycling process, then you will have them already. A full description of these items, together with instructions for making a mould and deckle can be found on pages 10–13. Additional items, required for the making of plant papers only, are described here.

Plant materials
Newspaper or absorbent paper
Mould and deckle
Liquidizer, or bucket and long, thick piece of wood
Oblong washing-up bowl or water tank
Shallow oblong tray
Smooth, reusable kitchen cloths
Two pressing boards 25 × 20cm (10 × 8in)
Palette knife
Clothes iron, optional
Alkaline solution, e.g. wood ash, washing soda, and caustic soda
Stainless steel or enamelled pot
Hotplate (portable stove)
Rubber gloves
Wooden, or heat-resistant plastic, spoon
Curtain mesh (window netting)

Alkaline solution

An alkaline solution is necessary in order to break down the plant material, releasing the cellulose fibres from the harmful acids and lignin which later will be washed away. Cellulose is a natural 'glue', occurring in most plants, which helps the fibres bond together when the paper is made. There are many alkaline substances available, such as wood ash, washing soda, soda ash and caustic soda. All of them will do the same job eventually, but the milder ones, e.g. wood ash, will take much longer to break down the plant material.

Wood ash is the least environmentally damaging material, and, provided that you have plenty of time and a little patience, this is the material that I would recommend you to use. However, there may be times when you wish to make very large quantities of paper, as I do frequently when carrying out commissioned work, and in these cases you may prefer to use a stronger solution, such as caustic soda, as a time-saving factor.

In this section the instructions for making the plant pulp use wood ash as the alkaline solution. If you decide to use a stronger substance, then please refer to the caution on page 34.

A selection of materials required for making plant papers.

Other equipment

You will need a stainless steel or enamelled pot in which to boil the plants and alkaline solution. It must not be aluminium or iron as the solution may react with the metal and damage the pot. If you are using an enamelled pot, then make sure that there are no cracks or chips in the glaze.

A hotplate is required on which to heat the alkaline solution. It is essential that your working area is very well ventilated during the cooking process because of the quantity of fumes given off. If you have access to a portable hotplate, or a small stainless steel boiler, then use this, and place it in a well ventilated area, preferably outside if the weather permits.

As a safety precaution, it is sensible to wear rubber gloves throughout the pulp-making process. A wooden or heat-resistant plastic spoon is needed to remove the plant material from the hot alkaline solution. Also, you will require a piece of curtain mesh (window netting) in which to hold the plant material whilst it is being washed. The mesh should be at least 60cm (24in) square and have a fairly close weave.

Caution

When using caustic soda as your alkaline material, please note the following:

- Always refer to and follow the manufacturer's guidelines or instructions for using the material.

- Be vigilant at all times and always wear rubber gloves when handling caustic soda as it can cause burns.

- To make a solution, use 1½ tablespoons of caustic soda to every 5 litres (1gal) of water. When dissolving the crystals in the water, stir the solution carefully to avoid splashing it.

- Never use an aluminium or an iron pot in which to boil the caustic solution as it will react with the metal and cause holes.

- Ensure that your working area is very well ventilated when boiling the solution. At best the fumes are foul smelling, and at worst they can be a health hazard.

- Never leave the boiling solution unattended. Being caustic, if it overflows, then it could cause a lot of damage to your hotplate.

- Disposal of this material can cause many problems, not least the pollution of rivers and water systems, so consider your choice carefully before deciding to use it.

- Although washing soda and soda ash are milder alkalis than caustic soda, it is wise to follow the above precautions when using any of these substances.

Choosing and preparing the plant material

Your choice of plant material will directly affect the type of paper that you produce. Paper can be made from most plants, and sometimes the least expected plants produce the strongest and best papers. In theory, it should be possible to make paper from anything that has been living at some time or other, the essential ingredient being cellulose fibre. However, in practice, some materials can prove extremely time-consuming and reluctant to be set as sheets of paper. If there is not enough cellulose, then the fibres will not bond together. If there is not enough fibre, then the paper will be low in strength, have a tendency to split easily, and warp whilst drying. The length of time that a plant is cooked, and the condition of the plant when cooked (whether it is freshly picked or decomposed) will all affect the resulting cellulose and fibre structures.

When choosing a plant with which to work, it is a good idea to consider the quantity of the plant available. This will be determined largely by the time of the year, unless you are using dried plants such as straw or hay. On average, you will need about one or two bucketfuls of

the plant material in order to make the process worthwhile. A good plant with which to start is grass, whether it be grass cuttings, reed grass, pampas-grass, or even something exotic like bamboo leaves if you can obtain them.

The photographs on pages 36 and 37 will give you some idea of the different plants that can be used and how the various papers might turn out. However, do not restrict yourself to these, but try anything that you can get hold of, provided that there is a sufficient quantity available.

Once the required amount of plant material has been gathered, it must be prepared before being placed into the alkaline solution. Remove any woody stems or tough stalks and make sure that the plant fibre lengths are no more than about 5cm (2in), by cutting them into strips.

Paper can be made from old cotton and linen sheets or rags. The best rags to use are those that are already falling apart and will tear easily. Tear them up into long strips and then tear the strips into 2.5cm (1in) squares, removing the less worn seams and stitching.

Preparing plant materials.

*A selection of plants suitable for
making paper.
1. Grass. 2. Maple leaves. 3. Nettles.
4. Dried dock leaves. 5. Foxgloves.
6. Ornamental pear. 7. Bark.
8. Bamboo leaves. 9. Rose petals.
10. Variegated privet. 11. Dried
leaves. 12. Hay. 13. Thistles. 14. Pine
needles.*

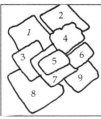

Papers from hedgerow plants.
1. Blossom. 2. Dock leaves. 3. Bamboo
leaves. 4. Springtime plants.
5. Thistles. 6. Grass. 7. Autumn
vegetation. 8. Pampas-grass.
9. Conifer needles.

1 △   2 △

Making the pulp

1. Having prepared your plants, the next step is to make an alkaline solution from wood ash. Make sure that the ash you use is 100 per cent wood ash, as the inclusion of any other burnt objects could affect the alkalinity of the material. Wearing rubber gloves, collect a bucketful of the ash and put it into a stainless steel or enamelled pot with about 5 litres (1gal) of water. Place this on your stove and bring it to the boil. Then, drain off the liquid through a fine sieve into another stainless steel or enamelled pot. This liquid is your alkaline solution in which you will boil your plants.

2. Put the plants into the liquid, ensuring that they are completely submerged. Cover the pot with a lid and place it on your stove. Turn the stove on to full power until the liquid boils, and then turn down the heat to a low simmer. It is very important not to leave the solution unattended, as it can overflow. To expel the fumes, make sure that the cooking area is well ventilated.

At this stage, if you wish to check upon the suitability of your plants, then wrap a small amount of each plant into a small bag of curtain mesh and place them all into the same alkaline solution. The colours might merge with each other, but it is a good way of finding out which plants are most suited to the papermaking process. Remember that different plants require different lengths of cooking time.

3 △

4 △

3. In order to establish when the plants are ready to use as a pulp, put your rubber gloves back on and, using a spoon, remove a small amount of the plant material from the pot. Squeeze some of the material between your gloved fingers; if it comes apart or feels very soft, then it should be ready.

Depending on the type of material that you use, the cooking time will vary greatly, e.g. fresh lawn grass will require a much shorter time than old cotton rags. Some materials may even require a further soaking time in a fresh alkaline solution in order to break them down sufficiently. As a very general guideline, when using wood ash as the alkaline solution, hedgerow mixtures, blossom, bamboo leaves, and pampas-grass heads need to be cooked for at least one hour. Thistles, potato plants, and straw need to be cooked for at least two hours, whilst seaweed needs to be cooked for a minimum of two hours and then soaked for at least twenty-four hours in a fresh solution.

4. Once the plants are ready, they have to be washed. Make sure that you have your rubber gloves on. Remove the pot and its contents from the hotplate. At this stage it is a good idea to add some cold water to the solution, in order to reduce the amount of steam coming out of the pot.

Take your curtain mesh and place it over an outside grid. Pour the liquid and plants from the pot into the mesh, making sure that no plant material escapes over the sides. When all the liquid has escaped through the mesh, pull up the corners to form a small bag in which to hold the plant material together.

5 △

6 △

5. Take the bag to a sink and wash the material thoroughly in running water. At first, a brownish dye will come out. Keep washing until the fluid coming out of the bag becomes clear.

6. Your plant material is now a pulp, and if you wish, then you can use it as it is to make paper. However, at this stage it is very likely that the pulp will produce a lumpy fibrous paper, possibly with some holes in it. In most instances it is preferable to pound or liquidize it before use. You can pound the pulp with a long, thick piece of wood in a bucket, or you can place it in a liquidizer for a few seconds. Pounding the paper will keep the fibres longer and, therefore, the final paper stronger, but it will obviously take more time than using a liquidizer.

If you decide to pound the material, then do this until the fibres break down completely, forming a consistent pulp. If you use a liquidizer, then you will find that a few seconds should suffice. This will keep some of the original pieces of plant material intact, making the paper more interesting. If a uniform, smoother paper is required, then liquidize the pulp for a longer period of time. Generally, you will require less pulp per unit of water when making a plant paper than when making recycled paper.

Full instructions for converting your pulp into sheets of paper can be found on pages 16–27.

Papers from seaweed. The different textural effects have been achieved by drying the papers by different methods (see pages 49–50).

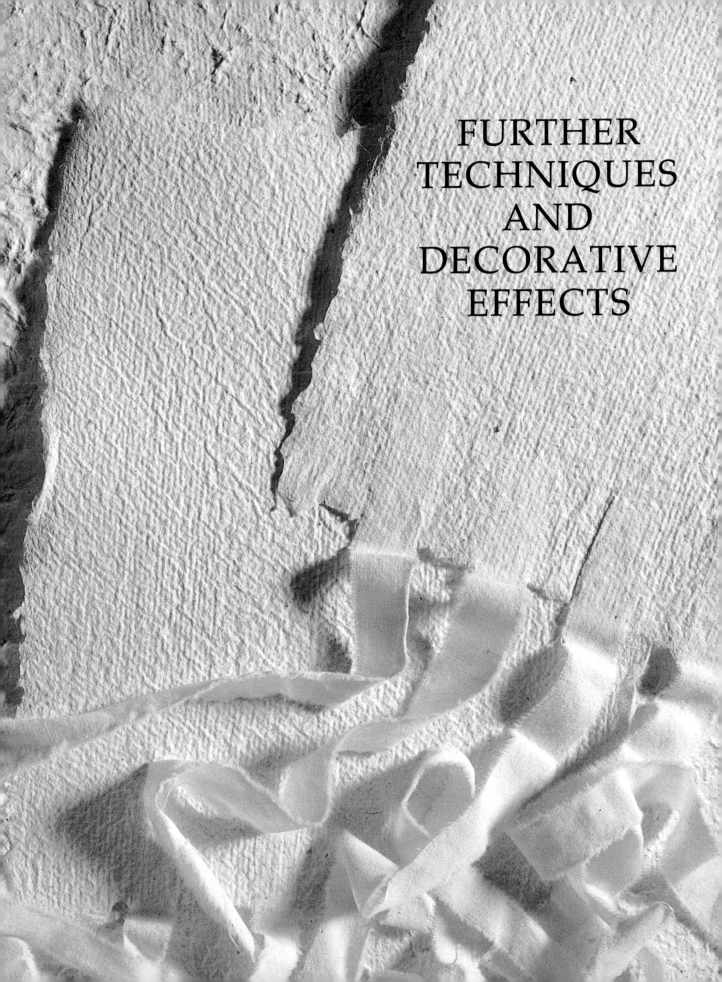

FURTHER
TECHNIQUES
AND
DECORATIVE
EFFECTS

Above: *bamboo leaves and cotton rags are both long-fibred raw materials suitable for making paper.*

Pages 42–43: *examples of two of the techniques that can be used to control the decorative and functional characteristics of paper. (Left to right) 1. Embossing. 2. Binding.*

Further techniques and decorative effects

Once you have mastered the basic process of making paper, either from waste paper or plant materials, you can move on to investigate some of the methods by which it is possible to control the functional and decorative characteristics of the paper. Depending upon the purpose for which your paper is being made, you may wish to improve its tensile strength, determine its texture, or alter its original colour. In this section I cover a variety of both functional and decorative techniques, ranging from water-proofing and dyeing the paper through to embossing it and binding it into simple books. Experiment with as many of these as you can, and you will soon begin to discover the enormous potential of the papermaking process.

Strengthening paper

The strength of your handmade paper will always be directly linked to the material from which it has been made. Therefore, choosing the best material with which to work is the golden rule.

With recycled papers, a poor quality news-print can only produce a lesser quality recycled paper. It will tear easily, yellow in sunlight, and eventually disintegrate. On the other hand, if you recycle a good quality cotton rag paper (watercolour paper), then you should end up with a strong and durable end result.

With plant papers, it is really a matter of experimentation to find the best material with which to work. At first, you may find it difficult to identify the best plants, but after a while you should become more familiar with their various characteristics, and this will tend to reduce the

risk of choosing unsuitable ones. A long-fibred plant rich in cellulose is usually a good choice. When making a plant paper, care must be taken at all stages, as any part of the process can damage the cellulose fibres. If the plants are cooked for too long or if they are liquidized harshly for long periods, then the strength of the final paper will be impaired.

In addition to selecting the most appropriate raw materials with which to work, you can use a variety of secondary strengthening materials in order to improve the strength of your handmade paper. Some of these materials are added at the pulp stage whilst others are applied to the finished paper, and they will all affect the paper in a different way.

A selection of materials used for strengthening paper: agar-agar flakes and strips; woollen and cotton fibres; shoe polish; candles; carrageen moss.

You may decide to add agents or chemicals to the paper, to make it waterproof, water resistant, or simply stronger. Alternatively, you may wish to improve the fibre content of the paper. This will increase the tensile strength of the paper and reduce the risk of it tearing. It is achieved by mixing longer fibres with the pulp, either using those from the original plant or by using cotton, string, wool or other plant fibres. Cut the fibres into shortish lengths, approximately 2.5cm (1in), and place them into the tank of liquidized pulp. Move the added fibres around in the tank to ensure that they are distributed evenly. It is advisable not to put the fibres into the liquidizer as they can become entangled in the blades and cause the motor to burn out.

Adding powdered starch to the tank of pulp.

Adding woollen fibres to the tank of pulp.

Stiffening the paper

The most immediate form of strengthening is to add size to the tank of pulp. There are a few different types of size that you can use. They will all increase the strength of the paper, as well as making it stiffer and, possibly, a bit crisper.

The size that is the easiest to obtain is a cold water starch, which can be purchased in powdered form. To start with, 1 or 2 table-spoons of powdered starch per 10 litres (2gal) of water should suffice. However, you can experiment with different amounts until the paper produced is to your liking. You may even try using the starch that is left in the water when you boil potatoes.

PVA (polyvinyl acetate) or rabbit skin glues are other possibilities. PVA glue is good, although it is a little more expensive than starch. It can be obtained from large hardware shops or art materials suppliers. Although it has been used commercially in the past, I have never used rabbit skin size myself. Apart from the fact that it produces foul smells and an unpleasant working environment, my own working practice is to avoid using animal products.

Strengthening the paper against water

This method of strengthening involves sizing again. This time the size is applied to the paper after it has been made and dried. It will stop the paper from acting like blotting paper and will also prevent it from falling apart in water. The materials that you can use include agar-agar (a gelatine made from seaweed and obtained from health food shops), ordinary gelatine, and carrageen moss powder (available from art and craft shops).

Agar-agar is the size that I use. Dissolve ½ teaspoon of the agar-agar in ¾ litre (1¼pt) of hot water. Pour this into a shallow tray and briefly immerse each dry sheet of paper into the mixture. Transfer the sized sheet onto a cloth and leave it to dry, weighting it with a book. Do not use heat to dry the paper as the gelatine will melt and stick to your cloth.

When using agar-agar, try to work quickly as the size will begin to set as it becomes cooler. If you have a metal tray, then you might be able to avoid this problem by keeping the tray and the gelatine mixture on a hotplate whilst dipping the paper.

Sizing the paper in an agar-agar solution.

Waterproofing the paper

This method of strengthening the paper also takes place after the paper has been made and dried. The object of the process is to try to get a sealing agent to penetrate into the paper, thus making it water repellent. This is ideal if you wish to make use of the paper outside, e.g. for envelopes, wrapping paper, or even for making kites! Materials that can be used as the sealing agent include waxed paper (sometimes used for wrapping food, and not to be confused with greaseproof paper), candle wax, shoe polish, varnish, and linseed oil.

If waxed paper is used, then place this paper, wax side down, on top of the handmade paper and cover them both with a sheet of brown wrapping paper. Using a medium heat, iron the back of the brown paper as evenly as you can, so that the wax is absorbed into the

Waterproofing the paper with wax.

handmade paper. Check the handmade paper frequently to ensure that the process is working correctly.

If candle wax or shoe polish is used, then rub the surface of your paper as evenly as possible with the wax or polish. Next, cover the paper with a sheet of brown wrapping paper and iron it so that the wax is absorbed into the paper. A spray wax polish can be used as an alternative.

Varnish, which affects the appearance of the paper most noticeably, is applied onto the surface of the paper with a brush and then simply left to be absorbed naturally.

Reinforcing the paper

The next method of strengthening the paper is termed sandwiching. This simply relies on reinforcing the paper with mesh, gauze or long strips of material.

Firstly, make your piece of paper and couch it onto your mound. You can now place any kind of material onto this piece of paper in order to reinforce its strength. Cotton, gauze, scrim (obtained from builders' merchants) or even wire netting can be laid upon the paper, depending on the strength required. Keep the strengthening material as flat as possible. Next, simply make another sheet of paper and couch this on top of the reinforcing material. It should bond to the sheet below as well as to the material, sandwiching the reinforcer between the two sheets.

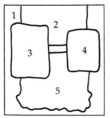

Textures created by the addition of secondary materials.
1. Recycled paper with twigs, seeds and other springtime plant material.
2. Recycled paper with bamboo leaves.
3. Recycled paper with lace and wool.
4. Recycled paper with paper strips.
5. Recycled paper with pieces of bark.

Texture of paper

For some time now, commercially produced papers have been supplied as smooth, flat, white sheets. It is possible to find some specialist papers, such as watercolour and etching papers, that have a more obvious texture. Usually, this texture has been made by the cloth or blanket onto which the paper has been couched and then dried, the surface of the cloth impressing itself into the paper. The texture of your handmade paper will be affected and determined by almost every one of the stages involved in its production.

The first thing that will have an effect is the raw material from which the paper is made. For example, if you select a very coarse plant material with which to work, then you must expect some difficulty in obtaining a paper with an eggshell surface.

The next influencing factor in the process is the method by which the raw material is pulped. If the pulping is done by hand, then a fairly coarse paper is likely to result, unless you have plenty of time and lots of patience. If a liquidizer is used, then the texture of the paper should be more even. When using a liquidizer, the main influence is the length of time that the material is liquidized. Generally, the longer that it is liquidized the smoother and more uniform the resulting pulp will be. For example, with plant papers the shorter the liquidizing time the more lumps and pieces of plant material there will be in the final paper. Although this can make the paper less functional, it does look very attractive. Similarly, when recycling paper the shorter the time of liquidizing the bigger will be the lumps of the original paper remaining in the pulp. This can be very useful for decorative purposes, especially when using two or more different coloured pulps in the same tank.

Any secondary materials that are added to the pulp, e.g. for strengthening purposes, will have an effect on the surface texture. Indeed, it is possible to add objects with the specific intention of altering the texture and appearance of the final paper. Tiny scraps of newsprint, pieces of wool, flower petals and

A range of different textured papers can be made from the same raw material, simply by treating it in different ways. The three papers shown here are all made from straw. (Left to right) 1. Paper made from cooked straw pulp, and dried by pressing. 2. Paper made from liquidized raw straw to which a minimum of pulp has been added, and dried on the mould. 3. Paper made from cooked straw pulp to which raw straw has been added, and dried on the mould.

seeds can all be used to create interesting and unusual textures.

The way that the pulp is applied to the mould will have a significant effect on the texture of the paper. Instead of using the tank, try pouring the diluted pulp straight onto the mould, letting it dry without pressing it. You will end up with a surface similar in appearance to a wave pattern.

Possibly the most influential part of the papermaking process is the way in which the paper is dried. If it is allowed to dry naturally on the frame, without removing it by couching,

then a variety of surface textures can be obtained. The pulp material will be allowed to form its own natural texture, revealing not only its contents but also the method by which it was applied to the mould.

As mentioned earlier, if the paper is couched and pressed onto a woven material, then the subsequent impression will remain on the sheet. This is a very simple way of imparting texture to a perhaps otherwise featureless pulp. Of course, the degree to which the texture is imparted will depend upon the method used to press the paper. Pressing by hand will not achieve as good a result as using a mechanical press such as a bookbinding press.

A heated clothes iron can be used to make the paper smoother, provided that it is used whilst the paper is still damp. Better still, you can use a trouser press. This is particularly useful when you have a large number of sheets to press and dry.

Above: equipment used for pressing paper: bookbinding press; clothes iron; electric trouser press.

Opposite: textures created by couching the paper onto a textured cloth.
(Top left to bottom right) 1. Embroidered piece of cloth. 2. Jute sacking. 3. Cotton cloth. 4. Woollen blanket. 5. Embroidered cloth with flower design.

An eggshell surface can be achieved by placing your couched and pressed piece of paper (still damp) onto a piece of Formica board or smooth metal to dry. Press out all the air bubbles with a damp kitchen cloth, using a rolling action and working from the middle of the paper outwards. When it is dry, peel the paper off, using a palette knife to ease the edges if you experience any difficulty in removing it.

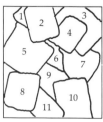

Freely-formed textures created either by drying the paper on the mould or by couching the paper and allowing it to dry on the couching cloth.
1. Recycled tissue with hay.
2. Recycled tissue with grass.
3. Recycled pulp mixture. 4. Computer paper. 5. Recycled tissue with grass.
6. Recycled paper with straw and a tea-bag dye. 7. Newspaper. 8. Straw.
9. Recycled paper with straw.
10. Bamboo leaves. 11. Recycled paper with wool.

Colouring and scenting

There are many ways of colouring your handmade paper. The most natural colour of all will come from the raw material itself, especially if it is plant based. Natural colours will tend to be earthy, e.g. brown, green, greeny yellow, browny red. Blue is very difficult to obtain naturally.

If you decide to use a secondary dye material, then this can be added either after the pulp has been liquidized but before it has been added to the tank of water, or just before the raw material is liquidized. If you choose the latter, then do not forget to wash your liquidizer when you have finished!

When considering which dye material to use, try at first to use whatever is at hand. Tea-bags are a good source. Ordinary tea gives a fairly strong brown colour if used in sufficient quantity, but some herb teas such as lemon verbena (cream) and rose hip (red) offer a wider range of possibilities. Add your tea-bags to boiling water and allow the tea to brew for as long as possible, stirring continuously in order to obtain as much dye as you can. Then, add this dye to your pulp before placing the pulp into the tank of water. If you are adventurous, then you could try making a dye solution from collected plants.

Brighter colours can be obtained from artificial dyes, the most accessible being coloured paper. If you simply add some pulped coloured paper to the liquidizer at the same time as your raw material, then you will change the original colour. Other possibilities include using inks and paints, and particularly vibrant colours can be obtained from fabric dyes.

If you wish to scent your paper, then you can add a strongly scented material, such as pot-pourri or herbs, to the pulp. Alternatively, you can simply apply some essential oils or perfume to the paper once it has been made and dried. This latter method will produce a stronger scent because it has not been diluted in water as in the first method.

A selection of materials that can be used for dyeing and scenting paper.

Embossing

Embossing is the process by which an impression or relief is formed on the surface of the paper. It is particularly useful for decorative purposes, and it can be used equally well to adorn a letterhead or to impart an impression over the whole sheet of paper. There are two ways of embossing paper, a wet method and a dry method.

Wet embossing

Wet embossing is the term used for the method which takes place during the process of making the paper. For the best result, the stage at which it should take place is after the sheet of paper has been formed on the mould and the deckle removed, but before couching takes place. As well as a variety of items with which to emboss the paper, you will need a flat sponge, two pressing boards, and a large woollen blanket, all at least 25 × 20cm (10 × 8in) in size.

Firstly, select some plastic or metal items that are reasonably flat, e.g. a linocut, string, a flat metal grid, or old wooden printing blocks, and place these onto your couching mound. Couch your newly formed sheet of paper onto the items, being careful not to press too hard. With a little practice, the sheet should remove itself cleanly from the mould. Next, remove your couching mound from beneath the newly formed sheet and replace it with a pressing board. Cover the sheet of paper with a clean cloth. Take your sponge and place it over the cloth, then cover this with the neatly folded blanket. Finally, add the last pressing board. Now, place it on the floor and simply jump up and down onto the top board, gently at first and then as hard as you can, being careful not to disturb the paper underneath.

Once you have applied as much pressure as possible, remove all the packing (sponge, blanket and pressing boards) and allow the paper to dry. When it has dried, peel the sheet off the cloth and remove the items which will be embossed into the paper.

After a few attempts, when your confidence has increased, try embossing some more difficult shapes. If you use uneven or odd-shaped items, then you may need more packing.

Dry embossing

Dry embossing is carried out once the paper has been made and dried. You will require a press, such as a bookbinding press, and a selection of flat, rigid items with which to emboss the paper, e.g. coins, keys or printing blocks. The method works best on paper that has been allowed to dry naturally on the mould. This produces a paper which is light to the touch, because no pressing has taken place. When pressure is applied to it selectively, by embossing it, the fibres will condense and form a clean impression. Mould-dried paper can take anything from one hour to a whole day to dry, so if you want to make any quantity of sheets to emboss, then you will need a number of moulds.

Once your sheet of paper has dried, place it onto a pressing board. Next, place your embossing item, face down, in the required position onto the paper. Cover this with another pressing board. Finally, place the 'sandwich' into your press and apply as much pressure as possible. When removed from the

Pages 54–55: a selection of papers dyed with natural and man-made materials.
(Left to right) 1. Tea-bag. 2. Lemon verbena tea-bag. 3. Hay. 4. Tea-bag. 5. Onion skins. 6. Dried leaves. 7. Sugar paper. 8. Blue sugar paper. 9. Red recycled paper. 10. Yellow fabric dye. 11. Green paper napkin. 12. Pink paper napkin. 13. Blue coloured paper. 14. Pink coloured paper.

A selection of objects used for embossing: metal grid; leaf; wooden and metal letterpress; nuts and bolts; coins; keys; linocut; string.

press, the paper should bear a clean impression of the item with which it has been embossed.

If you wish to emboss paper that has not been made specifically for this purpose and, therefore, has not been dried on the mould, then you will achieve the best result if you dampen the paper first. However, this can only be done safely if the paper has been sized (see pages 46–47).

A form of dry embossing actually occurs when a typewriter is used, the type impressing itself onto the surface of the paper at the same time as depositing ink in the shape of the given letter. The same effect can be achieved by using letterpress. This is an old form of printing where the letters are made individually from wood or lead. Sometimes, it is possible to obtain these letters from markets or second-hand shops. If you decide to use letterpress, then do not forget that you will still need a press in order to achieve a good impression.

Making watermarks

A watermark is an area of a sheet of paper where the pulp has been made deliberately thinner than in the rest of the sheet. When held against the light it will reveal a different density to the surrounding areas, allowing more light to permeate. Watermarks are often used by paper manufacturers in order to indicate their name or symbol on every sheet. You can incorporate any design that you wish into your handmade paper.

Traditional method

Commercially, watermarks are made by the addition of a metallic design to the mould. The design is made from copper and soldered onto the metal mesh of the mould. More than likely, your mould will have a nylon mesh and, therefore, you cannot solder a copper wire design onto it. Instead, you have to stitch it on.

Bearing in mind the size of your mould, start off by drawing a linear design on a piece of paper. Try to keep the design clear and simple, with as few lines as possible. Next, hold the design under the mesh, near the centre of the mould. Take some thin, pliable copper wire and stitch one end of it to the mesh, directly above any point on your design. Then, begin bending the wire to follow the design. After every 2.5cm (1in), and more frequently on curves, stitch the wire to the nylon mesh. When you have finished, try to cut off the excess wire as neatly as possible, as any stray pieces sticking out could damage the paper when it is made. Your watermark is now ready to use, and you can proceed with the paper-making process as normal.

The clearest watermarks will be obtained from very fine pulps that have short fibres. This can be achieved by keeping the pulp in the liquidizer until it is as fine and even as you can make it. Using a deckle will also help enormously, giving a greater contrast between the watermark and the surrounding areas, and also preventing holes appearing in the paper where the design repels the pulp too efficiently.

Opposite (top): an experimental watermark on a large sheet of paper. This is not a true watermark, although the result is quite effective. Strips of gummed paper tape were stuck onto the mould to act as a resist and prevent the pulp settling in these areas. However, when the pulp was applied the paper strips adhered to it, and when the dried sheet of paper was removed from the mould the paper strips came too.

Opposite (bottom): stitching copper wire onto the mould to create a watermark design.

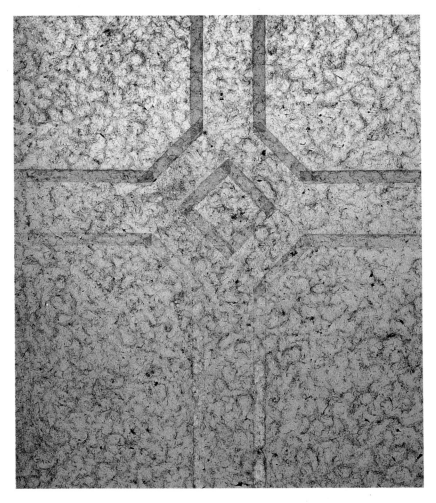

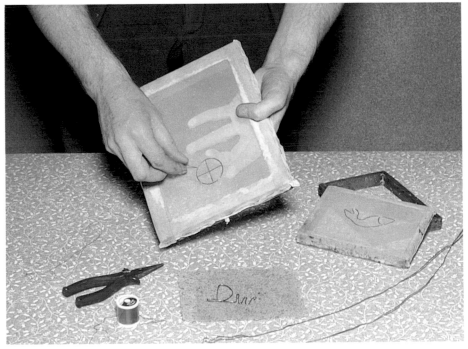

Traditional method adapted

The traditional method of making a watermark will give you the best and most clearly defined results. However, for the time that it takes to make the design, it is fairly limited in the design that can be created. A more complicated design can be achieved reasonably quickly by using materials other than copper wire, which can fulfil a similar role. PVA (polyvinyl acetate) glue can be used, provided that it is water resistant when dry. Alternatively, a waterproof wood glue can be used. Some of these glues are supplied in containers with thin spouts, and these are excellent for controlling the application of the glue. Follow the procedure used for copper wire, but, instead of bending and stitching wire to the nylon mesh, simply apply a thin stream of adhesive, following the lines of your design. You can make the line thicker and thinner according to the design that you are following. However, do not make it too thick as this will cause holes to appear in the sheet of paper when it is formed. It is best to keep the lines thin at first and then test the watermark by making a sheet of paper. If you think that it is possible to thicken the lines, then try it out.

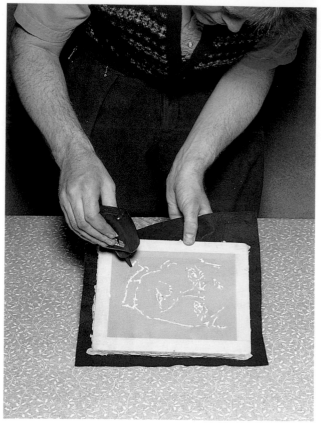

Spreading PVA glue onto the mould to create a watermark design. This particular design is a portrait of the author.

Under screen method

The disadvantage of the first two methods of making a watermark is that they depend upon the permanent application of a design to your mould, thus rendering it useless for anything else. However, there is an alternative method which does not involve changing the mould itself, and this is excellent for experimenting with different designs.

The watermark is achieved by holding an item underneath and against the mesh of the mould whilst you pull the mould through the tank to form the sheet of paper. As long as the item is sufficiently water repellent and flat then the process should work. Where the item touches the mesh either the pulp will not settle at all or it will be thinner than everywhere else. Whatever item is used to create the watermark, the edge that touches the nylon mesh must be flat.

If you can obtain them, then try using some old wooden printing blocks. Sometimes, they can be found at craft fairs or in ethnic and second-hand shops. Alternatively, you can try making blocks from lino or potatoes, cutting them into designs of your own choice.

Opposite (top and bottom): using the under screen method, a complex watermark can be created from an old textile printing block.

60

Making large sheets

Using the methods described so far in this book, that is, using a mould and deckle and a tank, it follows that the larger the sheet of paper that you wish to make, the larger your tank and your mould and deckle will need to be. The bigger the mould becomes the heavier it will be when pulled through the tank, due to the increased amount of water involved. Eventually, the point will be reached when the mould becomes so heavy and awkward to handle that it is impossible to remove it from the tank during the paper forming process.

There are a number of alternative methods by which it is possible to obtain large sheets of paper, each of which will produce a different effect. The object of these processes is simply to cover a large cloth, or the mesh of a large mould, as evenly as possible with pulp. The paper produced in this way will never be formed as evenly as paper that has been made on a mould and pulled through a tank.

Each of the processes will take a different amount of time. Usually, the longer the process takes the more even and flat the surface of the paper will be, the shorter the time then the more texture there will be on the surface. The best results are obtained by using a large mould which you have made and stretched yourself, but you can use a large blanket if it is not possible to make a mould. The paper produced on a blanket will not dry as quickly or be as flat as paper which has been produced and allowed to dry on a mould.

Baster method

The first method, which takes the longest amount of time but produces the smoothest paper, involves using a cookery baster. This tool is normally used to apply gravy to meat dishes, but I find it excellent for making large sheets. Being as careful and as patient as possible, apply the pulp to your mesh or cloth via the baster, until the whole surface has been covered. This will take you hours rather than minutes but, provided that you are careful, the results can be very good.

Applying pulp to the mould using a cookery baster.

Opposite: removing a large sheet of paper from the mould.

Applying pulp to the mould using a jug.

Pouring method

The second method simply involves pouring the pulp onto the mesh or cloth, using a jug or a spouted jar. The process is cruder than the baster method and, inevitably, you will end up with holes somewhere in the paper. However, if it is controlled carefully, then this method can be used to create a decorative paper which, from a distance, looks rather like lace.

Applying pulp to the mould using a hose.

Pouring method adapted

The third method is a refinement of the pouring method. If you can obtain a tank with a tap at the bottom, such as is used by wine or beer makers, then this will be ideal. Pour your pulp into the tank and attach a long hose to the tap. Turn on the tap and allow the pulp to come out of the end of the hose straight onto your mesh or cloth. This method will cover the surface very quickly but, generally, you will require a lot more pulp than when using the baster method. Also, the pulp must be fairly smooth, as any large lumps or pieces of plant material could become lodged in the hose and block the flow of pulp.

If you cannot obtain a tank with a tap, then you can try to siphon the pulp out of the tank by placing one end of the hose into the pulp mixture and sucking on the other end. Make sure that the bottom of the tank is higher than the end of the hose on which you are sucking. It is likely that you will get at least one mouthful of pulp before the liquid mixture starts flowing, but once it is flowing it will keep doing so until all of the pulp in the tank has been used up.

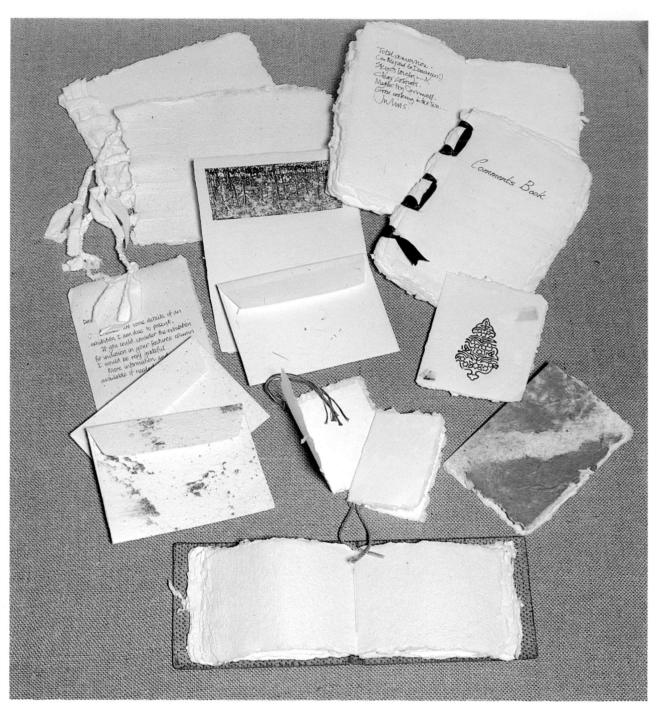

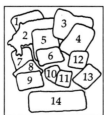

A selection of books, cards and envelopes made from handmade paper.
1. Book bound with cotton strips which have been threaded through holes in the paper and then tied. 2. Book bound with cotton strips which have been inserted during the papermaking process and then plaited together. 3,4. Books bound with ribbons. 5,6. Envelope, and writing paper with a photocopied design. 7,8,9. Envelopes and writing paper. 10,11. Gift cards. 12,13. Greetings cards. 14. Book bound with a linocut.

Binding

Bookbinding is a subject about which much has been written and there are many excellent books available. The simple bindings that are described here are intended only as an introduction, to show how paper can be bound quickly and effectively using materials that you are likely to have at hand.

The simplest type of binding can be applied to the paper whilst it is being formed. Firstly, form and couch a sheet of paper onto your mound, keeping it as thin as possible. Next, decide whether you wish to bind your paper into a landscape shaped book or a portrait shaped book. According to your choice, measure the width of the paper, and cut four lengths of thin twine, each measuring at least 15cm (6in) more than this width. Then, lay the four pieces of twine across the width of the paper, placing one near to the top, one near to the bottom, and two in between. Make sure that the distance between each of the pieces is about equal, and that the extra 15cm (6in) length of each one overhangs the same edge of the paper. Now make another sheet of paper on your mould and couch this on top of your strips of twine. The two pieces of paper should bond together and seal the twine between them. Continue making sheets in this manner until you have a sufficient quantity to make your book. You can start with as few as four, and there is no upper limit to the number that you can use.

Instead of using twine, you can try using an old cotton sheet which has been torn into thin strips. Because these strips are reasonably flat, they may not be as noticeable on the surface of the paper as twine. If you are not happy with the relief on the surface of the paper caused by the inset material, then you can use just two strips instead of four. Place these near to the top and the bottom of the sheet, leaving the middle area flat. Obviously, this binding will not be as strong as one which uses four strips.

Once all your sheets of paper with incorporated ties have dried, they can be tied together to form a book. Take two of the sheets and simply tie them together, using all four ties. Now take another two sheets and tie these together. Continue in this way until all the sheets are tied in pairs. Next tie two of the pairs together, then another two, and so on until all of the sheets are in groups of four. Tie one group of four to another group of four, and continue doing this until all of the sheets are in groups of eight. Join all the groups of eight to make groups of sixteen, then the groups of sixteen to make groups of thirty-two, and so on until all of the sheets are finally joined together. Clearly, the thinner the ties the easier it will be to tie a large number of sheets together.

A selection of binding materials: cotton scrim; jute scrim; cotton strips; bark; wool; ribbon; copper wire; cotton thread.

Objects from paper

Once you have familiarized yourself with the two-dimensional aspects of papermaking, you may wish to examine the potential of pulp as a three-dimensional medium. This is an area of papermaking which I am currently in the process of exploring myself.

To give you some ideas, I have illustrated a few examples of experimental three-dimensional pieces, most of which have been made more for fun than to fulfil any practical function. However, I feel certain that usable items can be produced from paper pulp, and I am sure that with a few minor changes, and perhaps a little more exploration, some of the examples shown here could be made to fulfil their intended function. Bear in mind that for centuries the Japanese not only made clothes such as kimonos from paper, but also used paper in conjunction with other materials to create lightweight armour for the samurai warriors. In my view, there is something intrinsically satisfying about being able to make items of clothing from materials such as grass cuttings!

If you are planning to use pulp for three-dimensional purposes, as a medium similar to clay, then you may need to utilize some of the functional techniques described earlier in this

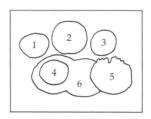

Casting experiments using paper pulp.
1,2. Recycled paper bowls cast from plastic bowls.
3. Recycled paper bowl cast from an old hat. 4. Recycled paper bowl cast from a sieve. 5. Cotton rag bowl cast from a plastic bowl. 6. Recycled paper doillies cast from plastic doillies.

section, e.g. one of the strengthening processes, before proceeding to make your object. It is also useful to discover some of the basic principles behind the methods that you intend using to create the item, e.g. casting, moulding or weaving. Obviously, the wider your knowledge the more you will be able to explore and, thus, exploit the medium. I hope that by experimenting with this aspect of pulp and paper, your view of both will be broadened.

A collection of experimental paper objects made from natural and recycled materials: brimmed hat by David Watson; scull cap by Lisa Poplett; square shopping bag by Amanda McLaren; triangular shopping bag by Rebecca Bell; waistcoat, necklace, and clutch bag by Wendy Jane Bravery.

PICTURES
FROM PULP

Above: The Science of the Soil.
This landscape was made for the cover of New Scientist *magazine, and from conception to completion it took two days to produce. It is made from recycled papers, stones, clay, plaster, wire, twigs, sea shells, miniature railway accessories, and a variety of other miscellaneous objects that were to hand at the time.*

Pages 70–71: Doone Valley, Exmoor, Devon.
Using a papermaking process, this landscape was produced entirely on location. It is made from plant materials (found at the site) and recycled papers, and it includes no inks or paints.

Pictures from pulp

The purpose of this section is to encourage you to explore the creative possibilities of pulp. Using simple drawing and patterning techniques, I show how pulp can be used pictorially, to express colour, texture and form. Despite the rather complex appearance of some of my landscapes, in fact, each one is simply a very highly textured piece of paper which has been allowed to dry naturally on the mould.

I started producing landscapes originally because of a desire to allow the materials that I use, i.e. plants, leaves, vegetables, and so on, to portray something of the atmosphere of their original location. When I depict a particular landscape, I try to capture its mood, not only by actually making it at the site itself, but also by using materials that I have collected from the site. The plants and pulp become my paint, a cookery baster my brush, and a mould my canvas. For me, the advantage of 'painting with pulp', as opposed to using more conventional materials, is that the colours and textures of the landscape do not have to be created; they are naturally inherent in the raw materials being used. In addition, the cellulose content of the pulp allows other objects, such as twigs and stones, to be incorporated into the picture without fear of them falling out.

I begin my landscape by choosing the area that I wish to depict. I may choose this site because of an interest in its historical significance, or simply because I feel attracted to its atmosphere. I visit the area several times to collect a variety of plants, trying as best I can to take only damaged or fallen materials. Also, for reasons which will become clear later, I try to find an accessible water supply.

Once back home, I prepare the plants and make a number of pulps. Then, I decide on the scale of the picture. Considering how heavy it will be when covered with pulp, I tend to use a mould no bigger than I can carry on my head or shoulder. Next, I drain the pulps and squeeze them into small balls to reduce their weight. Armed with as much equipment as I can carry, I return to the site to produce the final landscape. My list of equipment normally comprises the following: a mould; a selection of drained pulps; plastic jugs in which to mix the pulps with water (hence the need for an accessible water supply); a cookery baster; curtain mesh through which to drain any unused pulp; and a large cloth to cover the mould.

Once the landscape is finished, I cover it with a cloth to reduce the possibility of the pulp slipping on the mould whilst it is being carried home. If the picture does get slightly damaged during the journey, then provided that I have some of the original pulp left over, I am usually able to repair it.

Drawing with pulp

When drawing with pulp, the main piece of equipment that you need is a cookery baster. To start with, it is important that the pulp is of the correct consistency and this can only be gauged by trying to siphon some pulp up and into the baster. Obviously, if the pulp is too thick, then it will not suck up. If it is too thin, then it will be very difficult to apply it onto the frame. Experiment with it until you achieve the right consistency.

Preparing the coloured pulps.

well where they meet. Once you have completed the picture, you can either let it dry on the frame or, provided that it contains no objects such as stones or twigs, you can couch it onto a cloth.

Before you start your picture, it is worth preparing a number of pulps in a variety of colours and textures. It is not necessary to make the pulp by diluting it into a tank of water; simply pour it straight from the liquidizer into a jar or jug. When you have a sufficient amount of pulp, transfer it from the jar onto a mould, via your baster. If you wet the mould first, then this will help the water from the pulp to drain through it. When you apply the different pulps, make sure that they adhere

Patterning with pulp

This process is very similar to drawing with pulp. If you do not have a baster, then you can still achieve good results by using your hands, although the final appearance will be different. For this process, you will require a very thick pulp with a consistency similar to that of clay. This is produced by making a large amount of pulp and then drawing the water out of it using a sieve or some curtain mesh. Do not attempt to make a thick pulp simply by adding more raw material to your liquidizer, as this can cause the motor to burn out.

Once you have prepared all the different coloured pulps that you require for your picture, apply them to the mould with your hands, ensuring that their edges are joined together properly.

Drawing with pulp.

Patterning with pulp.

Couching the coloured sheets onto the cloth.

Making a patchwork

The object of this process is simply to cover a large blanket or cloth with a patchwork of different coloured pulps. As well as a large piece of cloth, you will require a number of different sized moulds, ideally ranging from very small to as large as your tank will take. If you have any round or odd-shaped frames, then these can be used too, for added interest. Also, you will need several tanks, each containing a different coloured pulp.

Firstly, select one of your moulds and a coloured pulp, and draw the mould through the tank of pulp to form a sheet of paper. Then, couch the newly formed sheet onto the large cloth, using the cloth as your mound. You may find this difficult at first, especially if the cloth is on a flat surface. However, if you wet the cloth thoroughly to begin with, then you should find it a little easier.

Repeat the process using a selection of different sized moulds and different coloured pulps until the whole cloth is covered. Make sure that all the sheets adhere to each other by overlapping them where they meet. If, at any stage, only half of a sheet of paper comes off the mould, then do not worry; the gap can simply be filled with another sheet.

A patchwork sheet of coloured pulps.

Above: The Faery Bridge, *Dunvegan, Isle of Skye, Scotland.*
This landscape is named after a Scottish folk-tale entitled The
Faery Bridge. *It was produced entirely on location, and it is
made from plants, stones and charcoal found at the site, and
recycled papers.*

Opposite (top): Doone Valley Woods, Exmoor, Devon.
*This landscape is made from plant materials (found at the
location) and recycled papers.*

Opposite (bottom): Arlington Beccott Woods, Exmoor,
Devon.
*This landscape is made from a mixture of plant materials and
recycled papers. It was produced as a preliminary study for the
picture shown on pages 78–79, to discover the characteristics
(strength, colour and texture) of the plant papers on drying.*

Arlington Beccott Woods, Exmoor, Devon.
A papermaking process was used to create this landscape, which
is made from plant materials (found at the site) and recycled
papers.

78

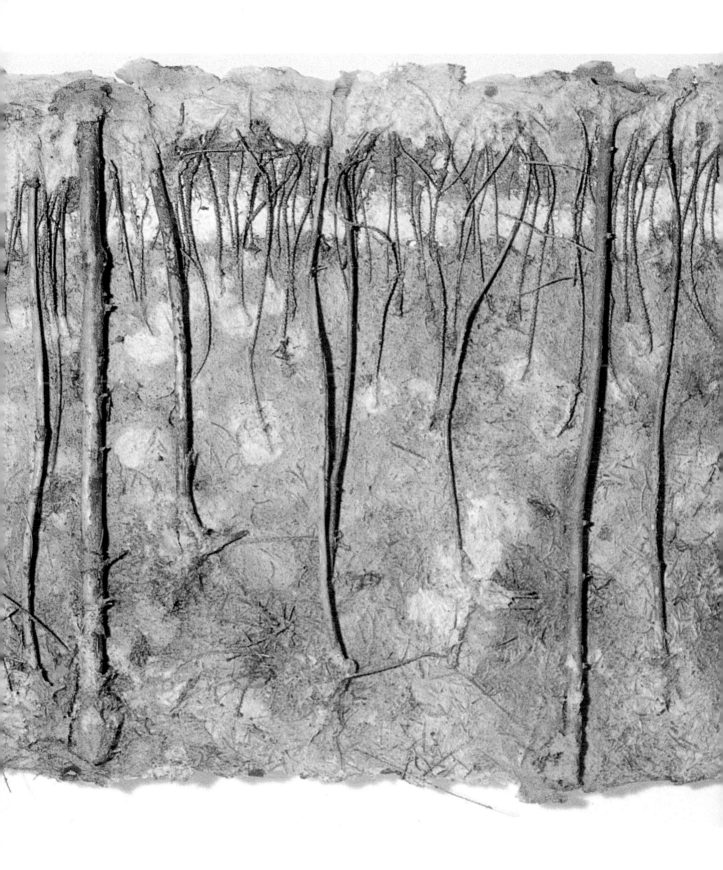

Index

If you have difficulty in obtaining any of the materials or
equipment mentioned in this book, then please write for further
information to the publishers: Search Press Ltd., Wellwood,
North Farm Road, Tunbridge Wells, Kent TN2 3DR